Understanding

SEXUAL
IDENTITY

Understanding
SEXUAL IDENTITY

A BOOK FOR GAY AND LESBIAN TEENS

AND THEIR FRIENDS

JANICE E. RENCH

Lerner Publications Company • Minneapolis

This book is available in two editions:
Library binding by Lerner Publications Company
Soft cover by First Avenue Editions
241 First Avenue North
Minneapolis, Minnesota 55401

LIBRARY OF CONGRESS CATALOGING-IN-PUBLICATION DATA

Rench, Janice E.
  Understanding sexual identity: a book for gay and lesbian teens and their
friends / Janice E. Rench.
    p. cm.
  Includes bibliographical references and index.
  Summary: Presents the facts in question and answer format about
gays and gay relationships, and what it means to a teenager who is
attempting to understand his or her own gay identity.
  ISBN 0-8225-0044-2 (lib. bdg.)
  ISBN 0-8225-9602-4 (pbk.)
  1. Gays—United States—Miscellanea—Juvenile literature. 2. Gay
teenagers—United States—Miscellanea—Juvenile literature.
[1. Homosexuality. 2. Questions and answers.] I. Title.
HQ76.26.R46 1990
306.76′6—dc20   90-38073
                                                            CIP
                                                             AC

Manufactured in the United States of America.

  2 3 4 5 6 7 8 9 10 99 98 97 96 95 94 93 92

Acknowledgments

It is with my deepest respect and gratitude that I acknowledge the following people and organizations, both gay and nongay, who supported my efforts in writing this book.

To my editor, LeeAnne Engfer, for her personal support, technical assistance, and thoughtful editing.

To those professionals who have worked tirelessly to educate and offer love and support to others: Kevin Berrill, Director, Anti-Violence Project of The National Gay and Lesbian Task Force, Washington, D.C.; James T. Brock, Pastor, Joy Metropolitan Community Church, Orlando, Florida; John Nolan, AIDS Commission of Greater Cleveland, Cleveland, Ohio; Dolores L. Noll, Acting Executive Director, and Aubrey Wertheim, Director of Services, Lesbian/Gay Community Service Center of Greater Cleveland, Cleveland, Ohio; Leo Treadway, Ministry Associate, St. Paul-Reformation Lutheran Church and adult leader of gay and lesbian youth groups.

To those very special friends who contributed ideas, support, and encouragement: Lilli Brock, Susan Clifford, Gloria Crosby, Brent Erdmann, Barbara Hartford, Mary Ann Salerno, Pat Sarty, Gina Solano, and Ellie Strong.

With thanks and appreciation to my husband, Larry, for his ongoing support, love, and caring.

*With love
to Al and Darryl*

CONTENTS

FOREWORD

All through my childhood I felt different from most other kids around me. But it wasn't until adolescence that my sense of being different came into focus. Slowly it hit me. "Oh my God," I thought, "I'm queer."

Everything I had heard about "queers"—in conversations, in books, and in the media—carried the message that they were sick, sinful, predatory, depraved creatures who were incapable of loving or being loved. But there was hope. Back then the newspaper advice columnists were still proclaiming that homosexuals could become heterosexual if they wanted to. I *wanted* to be heterosexual and was determined to become one. Moreover, I vowed that if I was still "queer" by the time I was 17, I would hang myself with a necktie.

But something happened between then and now. I got the facts. I learned that homosexuality, while not the norm, is normal. I discovered that it has nothing to do with hating or fearing the opposite sex or molesting children, and everything to do with loving and being loved. Most importantly, I met gay people who shattered the stereotypes. Ever so slowly, I have come not only to accept but also to affirm who I am.

Had I not had gay role models or access to accurate information about homosexuality, the story of my life would have been much different—and probably much shorter. Thanks to the courage of openly gay people and supportive heterosexuals, I have been able to embrace my gay identity.

But many others are not so fortunate. Research suggests that lesbian and gay youth are much more likely to attempt or commit suicide than are heterosexual youth. This is a consequence of the enormous stress of growing up in a society that teaches gay people to hide and to hate themselves.

In addition, there is evidence that antigay harassment and violence have reached epidemic proportions. Such abuse occurs in all kinds of situations, including on the street, in schools, in churches, and even in the home.

This informative and sensitive book challenges the ignorant assumptions that lead to discrimination and even violence against gay people. Moreover, it contains information that will help heterosexual readers to understand and support gays and lesbians. Most importantly, it gives those who are discovering their lesbian, gay, or bisexual identities an opportunity to not only accept but also celebrate who they are.

Kevin Berrill, Director
Anti-Violence Project
National Gay and Lesbian Task Force
Washington, D.C.

INTRODUCTION

Understanding and accepting people who act or think differently or look different from us is essential for a more tolerant and nonviolent society. Understanding the many aspects of human behavior can be a confusing task, particularly when information is withheld. This is especially true when we talk about sexuality.

Our sexuality can be looked at in two different ways. First, we can learn about the physical side of sex—who does what to whom, what feels good, what we don't like, and who we want to be sexual with. Second, and just as importantly, we need to understand the emotional part of sexual attraction: what is love and what are the feelings that accompany a sexual relationship?

In this society, we learn about romantic relationships from people around us, such as parents, friends, and neighbors, and from movies, television, books, and music. Usually we see and hear about heterosexual relationships— those between boys and girls or between men and women. Most of us grow up believing that heterosexual relationships are the only right or natural relationships between people. We assume that everyone is heterosexual.

The wonderful thing about humans is that we are not all the same. The human race is like a tapestry, with each thread representing the uniqueness and beauty of each individual. This uniqueness is reflected in every aspect of our lives, including our sexuality. Many people feel physical attraction to and romantic love for someone of their own gender. Studies show that at least one person in ten is gay. This is true for all cultures and in all periods of history.

In *Loving Someone Gay*, Don Clark writes, "We're like that beautiful orange flower called the California poppy. We are apt to pop up anywhere—beside a railroad track, in the wilderness, in a pampered floral display, or in a long forgotten garden covered with weeds and trampled by careless footsteps. We keep blooming with a beauty that is there to be seen by anyone willing to appreciate it." Clark was referring to our neighbors, relatives, and friends who are gay or lesbian. Gay men and lesbians interact with heterosexual people at home, in the classroom, at work, on sports teams, in church, and everywhere else that people get together to work or socialize.

Sexuality is a complex, fascinating subject, but one that many people don't feel comfortable discussing openly. There are many myths about homosexuality in particular. Unfortunately, most of these myths are degrading and describe gay people as abnormal, mentally ill, or dangerous to society. Many people who believe these myths do not know any gay men or lesbians.

This book will not try to determine your sexuality, but it will attempt to dispel some of the myths about gay and lesbian people. Hopefully, young readers who are not gay will begin to understand some of their prejudices and fears. They will strive to become comfortable with differences and work against violence, hatred, and ignorance. Young gay and lesbian readers will realize that they are not abnormal and they are not alone—many people have experienced the same feelings they have. They will learn how to better understand their sexual identity.

CHAPTER ONE

Facts about Homosexuality

Clank, clank, clank, riiiiiing, clank, clank, clank. The sound of slamming lockers echoed in the hallways as students rushed to get to their next class.

"Come on, Brewster, move it, you're going to be late for class again," bellowed Mr. Novack as he held open the door. The last bell had just rung. When the door was closed, Mr. Novack would mark Brian late for class.

Brian moved closer into his locker, which was across the hall from Mr. Novack's English classroom. He hated the way the male teachers, especially Mr. Novack, called him by his last name. He said it in a sing-song, mocking way, emphasizing BREW and stringing out S-T-E-R, so it came out like a question: "BREW SIR?"

One day last fall when Brian was in the cafeteria, a boy in his class had come up to him. Sweeping his arm through

14

the air and bowing at the waist, the boy had asked in a loud and mimicking voice as he held out a cup, "Brew, sir?" It was silent in the cafeteria as they stood there. Brian couldn't move. He felt like everyone was looking at him. His face burned and it seemed like there was cotton in his mouth. Then he heard laughter coming from every corner of the cafeteria. Brian stood frozen to the spot until finally he felt bodies bumping into him as the kids hurriedly left the cafeteria. Some of the girls giggled, and the boys called him "faggot" and "homo." The words rang in his ears as he ran from the room.

Brian was a pale, thin boy with large, dark eyes and thick, straight hair that was cut shorter than the fashion. He was growing so fast that most of his pants were too short. The kids teased him about wearing "flood pants." He tried to hide his height by walking with his head down and his shoulders hunched, his eyes glued to the floor.

Ever since the incident in the cafeteria, school had been unbearable. People called him a "faggot" and threatened to "kick his queer behind one of these days." That's why he was stalling now. He felt safer arriving in class after the teacher was in the room.

As Brian gathered up his books, he remembered the poem his mother had taught him when he was little—"sticks and stones may break my bones, but names will never hurt me." It used to help to say it, he thought, but not anymore.

Does name-calling really hurt anyone?

Words are very powerful and can be used hurtfully. Being called names that are shameful or demeaning, especially if it happens over a long period of time, can affect the way we feel about ourselves. For example, if your parents or teachers tell you that you're stupid, lazy, or ugly, you might eventually start to believe it. Being called names can also make you feel like an outsider. This is particularly difficult in the teen years, when belonging to a group and being liked by your peers is very important.

What do "faggot" and "homo" mean?

Faggot and *homo* are slang words used to describe a man who is gay. The term *faggot* may have come from the word *fagot*—a stick of wood used to start a fire. During the Middle Ages, gay people were considered dangerous and were sometimes burned at the stake. *Homo* is an abbreviation of the word *homosexual*, which means attracted to someone of the same sex. The first part of the word comes from the Greek word *homos*, or "same." The term *queer* is used to denote something different or odd. *Lesbian* originally referred to people from the Greek island of Lesbos, where the poet Sappho lived. Since Sappho wrote poems about love between women, gay women eventually came to be called lesbians. A slang term used to describe a lesbian is *dyke*, a word that stems from the 19th-century word *dike*, which referred to male clothing. The words *faggot, fag, queer, dyke, homo,* and *lesbo* are usually considered derogatory, or insulting.

Sometimes, as in Brian's story, the words are used in a hurtful way against anyone who appears to be different.

What is a lesbian or gay person?

A lesbian is a woman who feels emotional and sexual affection towards another woman. A gay man feels emotional and sexual affection towards another man. A male homosexual is generally referred to as "gay" and a female as "lesbian." Some people are physically and emotionally attracted to men and women—they are bisexual.

What kinds of people are lesbian or gay?

Gay and lesbian people have existed in every society since the beginning of recorded history. All kinds of people are gay and lesbian: young, middle-aged, and old people; black, white, Hispanic, Native American, and Asian; lawyers, doctors, teachers, clergy, actors, dishwashers, business executives, athletes, police officers, mothers, fathers, brothers, sisters, friends, and grandparents. Gay people are represented in every occupation and segment of society.

Some famous gay or bisexual people include: Gertrude Stein (U.S. writer), James Baldwin (U.S. writer), Pyotr Tchaikovsky (Russian composer), Hans Christian Andersen (Danish writer), Martina Navratilova (Czech tennis player), Dag Hammarskjöld (U.N. secretary-general), Andy Warhol (U.S. painter), Tennessee Williams (U.S. playwright), David Bowie (British singer), Rock Hudson (U.S. movie star), Willa Cather (U.S. writer), Janis Joplin (U.S. singer).

In the past, many gay and lesbian people chose to hide their sexual identity. More and more movie actors, athletes, and politicians are coming forward about their sexuality.

How many gay and lesbian people are there?

According to sexual behavior researchers William Masters and Virginia Johnson, ten percent of the population (one out of every ten people) is probably gay or lesbian. You might not realize it, but chances are that one of your acquaintances or someone in your family is gay.

Can you tell by looking at someone that he or she is gay?

Some people believe that you can tell simply by the way someone walks, dresses, or talks, or by what kind of job he or she chooses, that the person is gay. To judge anyone by such limited information is unfair, however. It is also usually incorrect.

Although society is changing, there are still many stereotypes used to describe males and females. For example, men are supposed to act strong and not show emotion. Women are supposed to be quiet, with a soft look and manner. When men and women behave or dress in ways that go against the traditional gender roles, people often assume that they are gay. When a man shows "feminine" characteristics, he is often thought to be gay. If a woman dresses or acts in what is considered a masculine manner, she might be assumed to be a lesbian.

Actually, all of us have masculine and feminine characteristics. Stereotyping limits our natural feelings and actions. To say that all male hair stylists are gay because we think of hairdressing as a feminine profession is limiting to men and women. Similarly, it's wrong to assume that all female gym teachers are lesbians because some people think of sports as a masculine profession. Both heterosexual and gay people often defy gender stereotypes to express their personalities and abilities.

What do gay couples do together?

Many people are curious about what gay couples "do" together sexually. In fact, people often view gay men and lesbians in just one dimension—sexual. Being homosexual, heterosexual, or bisexual involves much more than sex, however. Sexual identity also has to do with love, relationships, and one's lifestyle.

Like heterosexual couples, gay couples enjoy each other's company in a variety of activities, such as work, sports, hobbies, classes, and through worship at their church or synagogue. When two people feel emotionally close, trust each other, and are physically attracted to one another, they may want to have a sexual relationship. Basically, all human beings do a variation of the same things for and to each other in a sexual relationship, such as kissing, touching, caressing each other's body, and holding each other close.

Because of the tendency to think of couples in heterosexual terms, people sometimes ask gay and lesbian couples, "Who plays the man?" or "Who plays the woman?" Again, these questions are based on stereotypes about gender and sex roles. These traditional roles are not a part of most gay relationships.

What are some of the myths about gays and lesbians?

There are many myths about the way gays and lesbians live. For example, some people believe that gay men are child molesters. The truth is that more than 90 percent of all convicted rapists and child molesters are heterosexual males.

Another myth is that adult lesbians and gays try to convince or "recruit" young people to become gay. The fact is that people can't change their sexual identity or orientation. A gay person cannot be forced to become heterosexual, and a heterosexual person cannot be convinced to become homosexual. Actually, the pressure from the heterosexual community to conform to a heterosexual orientation continues to be very strong.

Some people think it is against the law to be lesbian or gay. This is not true. No such law exists in any state. Some states have laws about how homosexual (and heterosexual) people can behave sexually. But being gay or lesbian involves more than just sexual behavior.

It is also a myth that gay men hate women and that lesbians hate men. Gay people have friends of both sexes, and many gay men and lesbians socialize together and work together on political issues.

What is homophobia?

Homophobia is defined as the fear or hatred of lesbians and gay men. Homophobia can take many forms, such as name-calling and verbal insults, avoiding gay people, verbal and physical harassment, or even violence.

Many homophobic attitudes stem from an early religious belief that people should only engage in sexual activity for the purpose of reproduction—having children. Since gay men and lesbians cannot produce children through sexual intercourse, their relationships were seen as existing solely for pleasure. Therefore, some people believed that homosexuality was a sin against God and the community.

Another idea that leads to homophobia is that people who are different are a threat to society. Those individuals who do not follow what the majority of people in society believe is right are suspected of trying to destroy society. Some people think that lesbian and gay relationships pose a threat to the traditional family.

Like all forms of prejudice, such as racism, sexism, and

ageism (discrimination against older or younger people), homophobia separates us as human beings. It denies the self-worth and unique potential of each of us and robs all of us of our dignity.

CHAPTER TWO

Friends

Leslie waved as she ran toward her friends in the school yard. As she got closer, she could hear the song her friends were singing about her and Tony—"Leslie and Tony sitting in a tree, k-i-s-s-i-n-g, first comes love, then comes marriage, then comes Leslie with a baby carriage."

Ever since Tony had asked Leslie to be his partner in a science project, the kids had been teasing them both about "going together." She knew the kids were just trying to get her riled up, but the teasing did make her think about all those things the girls were talking about at pajama parties and in the rest room—boys, kissing, and "doing it." She didn't understand why they just couldn't call it "having intercourse," because that was what they meant.

She had known about intercourse since the fourth grade, when her best friend, Felicia, had told her what men and women did together. She and Felicia made a promise to each other that they would never have intercourse with *any* boy. To make sure the promise would never be broken, they had conducted a ceremony in Felicia's backyard. Leslie brought the Bible from her house. They put their hands on the Bible and swore to always stay together and never to have intercourse with any boy. Then they kissed and hugged each other.

"Yuck," she thought as she slowed down her pace, "I could never kiss Tony—or anyone else for that matter." It wasn't that she didn't like Tony. He was a real nice kid. He was the only one who would listen to her talk about science. Science was her favorite subject, but everyone thought she was "weird" when she talked about being a scientist.

"You're only 11, Leslie, you have plenty of time to decide what you want to do with the rest of your life," her mother would say, patting Leslie's head as if she were a dog. Her mother also said that Leslie was just going through a phase of not liking boys.

"How do you think you'll ever find a husband if you have your nose stuck in a test tube all day?" her father would ask, usually from behind a book.

"I want to live with Felicia and I want to be a scientist," Leslie told her parents. "In fact, maybe I'll be the first scientist to figure out a way for men to have babies, so no one would ever have to have intercourse again!"

The thought of a man with his pregnant belly sticking out made her laugh out loud as she ran faster to catch up with her friends.

Are kids who spend a lot of time together gay?

Friendships take many forms, and wanting to spend time with someone of the same sex does not necessarily mean you are gay. Children show a preference for same-sex friendships as early as the age of three. Young children enjoy the good feelings that touching and hugging their friends bring —they aren't concerned about the gender of the friend. During the early childhood years, hugging, kissing, and holding hands with a same-sex friend are accepted and even considered "cute." But as we grow up, we begin to learn what is culturally acceptable. Unfortunately, in our culture, most people are not comfortable with males openly showing affection toward each other.

Many heterosexual people feel attracted to someone of the same sex at some point in their lives. In early adolescence, it is common to have a crush on someone of the same sex. These crushes are normal and often have little to do with sex.

Adolescence is also the time when many gay and lesbian people begin to recognize their feelings for their own sex and to question whether something is wrong with them. Many people say they knew they were gay even before they had a name for their feelings.

If I have sexual dreams about my best friend, am I gay?

Dreaming about someone you like and spend a lot of time with is normal whether you are homosexual or heterosexual. Most people test and explore many feelings and ideas during adolescence. For example, as a teenager you might try smoking or you might experiment sexually.

Even if you have sex with someone of the same gender as a teenager, it doesn't necessarily mean that you will have a gay sexual identity as an adult. Usually it will be clear to you if you enjoy being sexual with someone of the same gender.

How do you become gay, lesbian, or heterosexual?

No scientific research completely explains how or why people are sexually attracted to each other. Some possibilities that have been suggested over the years include how a person was raised by his or her parents, biological makeup, prenatal (before birth) factors, or some combination of these factors. Most researchers do agree that first, individuals do not choose their sexual orientation; that sexual orientation is established very early in life (before the age of five); and finally, that although it is possible to ignore one's feelings or expression of sexual identity for a while, it doesn't work over a long period of time. Since being gay, lesbian, or bisexual is not an illness, you can't catch it and there's no "cure" for it. Trying to cure or change someone's sexual identity will only make that person unhappy.

If I spend time with a gay friend, will I become gay?

Spending time with a gay friend, brother, sister, or parent does not mean you will become gay. Nor will his or her influence make you want to change your own orientation. A friend who lets you know that he or she is gay is sharing a very important part of himself or herself with you. This kind of trust can be the basis for a very special friendship. It's really a compliment to you that your friend trusts you so much!

If I'm a boy who doesn't like sports or a girl who doesn't like wearing makeup, does that mean I'm gay?

No. It only means that you have unique interests and ideas. Many people, especially teens, go along with the crowd just to fit in. Sometimes it takes special courage and strength to be different. It is your right to choose those things that fit your personality and bring you pleasure. While your peers' opinions are important, they are not as important as being honest about who you are.

CHAPTER THREE

Families

"Look at those queers with their arms around each other. What is this world coming to anyway? They should be rounded up and put in jail. That's what I would do if I was running the city."

"Oh Joe, what a terrible thing to say. They're just kids . . ."

"Oh Joe, baloney," he loudly interrupted, mocking his wife. "That's what's wrong with this world. Women don't know how to be women—look at them," he shouted, pointing to the television. "No wonder they can't get a man to marry them. They don't even look like women. A bunch of dykes and fairies, that's what they are."

Joe shifted in his chair and reached for the television remote control, sighing as if he held the weight of the world on his shoulders. The newscasts on all the stations were reporting the gay and lesbian march on Washington.

"Joe, what if our Timmy or Angie was one of those kids marching," asked Nancy, "you wouldn't want them arrested, would you?"

"No kid of mine would ever be a homo!"

"But Joe, let's say Angie came to us and told us she was a lesbian?"

Joe jammed the lever on the side of his recliner chair and jerked forward. He stood up from the chair, making it clear that the discussion was over. His face was flushed. As he left the room, he said angrily, "I would disown any kid of mine that wanted to live that kind of life."

Is Joe's reaction common?

Unfortunately, some parents react with anger or hostility to the idea that their children might be gay. Some parents are even violent. There may be several reasons for a negative reaction. Parents may feel guilty or responsible in some way for their child being gay or lesbian. "Where did I go wrong?" is a common question parents ask. They might be afraid that their friends, neighbors, and relatives will not accept them or will judge them as unfit parents. Also, parents might think, "We will never have grandchildren," or "My son or daughter will live a lonely, sad life without anyone to love them." Perhaps the parents' religious group does not accept the idea of homosexuality. Parents, like gay and lesbian people themselves, are often surprised by the discovery of homosexuality. Most know little about it. To fill in the information gap, they fall back on myths and stereotypes.

Most parents need time and support to understand their child's sexual orientation. Just as gay men and lesbians may take several years to accept their sexual identity, families and friends also need time. It is natural for parents to feel some anger, sadness, and confusion at first.

Do some parents really disown their children because they are gay or lesbian?

Because of a lack of information, some parents may disown—completely reject—their son or daughter. Sometimes one parent will not accept the child, while the other one will. Many more parents work through their initial reaction of anger or shock and establish a wonderful relationship with their gay son or lesbian daughter. If there has been discussion and mutual respect between the child and the parents in the past, parents will likely accept their child's sexual identity and offer their support. Most parents want the best for their children and want them to be happy.

Why do gays and lesbians want to draw attention to themselves by marching?

Gay and lesbian people, like other minorities who have been discriminated against, find strength in publicly joining together. Gay people demonstrate to gain basic civil rights, so that they cannot be fired from a job, for example, or be kicked out of an apartment because of their sexual identity.

One of the most significant events for gay people happened during the summer of 1969 in New York City. After years of enduring harassment, beatings, and killings, gay people fought back. When police raided a gay bar called the Stonewall, the patrons resisted and a riot broke out. The event came to be known as the "Stonewall Rebellion." Throughout the country, marches each year commemorate that date and celebrate Gay Pride Day. Another important event was the 1987 March on Washington, in which between 250,000 and 750,000 gay men and lesbians gathered in the capital to demonstrate for gay civil rights.

Do these marches really help anyone?

Gay pride marches help all of us in many ways. It feels good—self-affirming—for people to declare publicly, "I am a gay or lesbian person and I will no longer hide and pretend to be something I'm not. I will not remain silent about who I am." Public marches also force the rest of society, through media attention, to acknowledge the existence of gay people. This acknowledgment is a first step toward breaking down prejudices and fear.

Do gay and lesbian couples have children and families?

Gay and lesbian couples do establish families. In fact, any two people who live together and love and care about each other can create a family. The traditional definition of family is changing. The nuclear family (mother, father, children) is just one kind of family unit. Other kinds of families include stepparents, single parents, and adopted children. Gay men and lesbians may also have children. For example, Jeannie and Alice, a lesbian couple who had lived together for seven years, decided to have a child. Jeannie was artificially inseminated. This means that semen from a male donor was inserted into her womb. Jeannie went through a natural birth process, and Alice was with her at the birth. Together they are now raising their son. Jack and Tom are also gay parents. Jack had been married, and he and his wife had had a son and a daughter. After Jack and his wife divorced, they agreed to have joint custody of the children. The children stay with Jack and Tom during school months and spend summers with their mother.

My oldest brother is gay—does that mean I will be too?

Having a gay brother or a lesbian sister does not mean that you will be gay too. Remember, being gay is not an illness; it's not contagious. You don't have to treat your brother as if he is different. Talk openly about your feelings and learn about his. Respect his privacy about who he wants to tell or not tell that he is gay. If your parents are having a difficult time accepting the information that your brother is gay, try to remain supportive yourself. You can feel glad that your brother trusts you enough to tell you about his gayness.

Is there somewhere relatives and friends can go for information?

A national group called Federation of Parents and Friends of Lesbians and Gays (P-FLAG) has 200 chapters throughout the U.S. and Canada. The group's mission is to help families understand homosexuality. (See page 52 for information about how to find the P-FLAG chapter in your area.)

CHAPTER FOUR

Religion

Eric lay on his bed humming the tune to the song he had learned in Sunday School, "Yes, Jesus loves me, yes, Jesus loves me, yes, Jesus loves me, for the Bible tells me so." It was such a comforting song, he thought as he remembered the mornings he had spent with his friends in Sunday School while his parents sat with the other adults in church. The only time the kids were allowed in the big church with their parents was during the Christmas and Easter celebrations. Those were special times for him. He had enjoyed watching the older boys up at the altar helping the minister. Eric had been anxious to become an altar boy himself.

There was one boy in particular who Eric remembered seeing when he was seven years old. The boy, dressed in a white robe that contrasted with his dark hair and fair skin, looked handsome standing by the altar holding the cross.

After that, each Sunday Eric would take the back way to his Sunday School class, past the room where the altar boys were changing. When he was able to catch a glance of the boy, Eric felt good inside. For the rest of the day he would think about the boy and fantasize about them being friends. This Sunday morning ritual went on for almost a year.

Why was he remembering all this now, after eight years, he wondered, moving onto his back and staring up at the ceiling. He knew why, but to admit it even to himself, after what the minister had talked about last week, was scary.

Eric had tried hard to be a good person. He studied hard in school and was among the top five in his class. He played clarinet in the band and was an altar boy at church. The girls thought he was cute and he had gone steady with one of them. He had even continued going to Sunday School when most of his friends would skip out and go to the mall to play videos.

But in the last few months, Eric was finding he couldn't hold back his physical attraction to a boy he had met at band practice. Then, last week during Bible discussion, the minister talked about how sinful homosexuals were and how they would be punished for their unclean thoughts and immoral ways. Eric felt scared. He decided that he'd better not ever tell anyone how he felt about that boy. He would work harder at being a better person and maybe he wouldn't be punished by God.

Could Eric change the way he felt?

Eric could not change his feelings of attraction to men any more than someone who has feelings for a person of the opposite sex can. Gay and lesbian youth often feel pressure to change. They might think that they should have "clean" thoughts and show more self-discipline. They might date someone of the opposite sex, hoping this will change their sexual feelings. They may hope to "grow out of" those feelings. Young gay people often feel unpopular or unattractive because they do not share their classmates' feelings about dating, sex, and social events. They might end up feeling guilty, worthless, and without self-confidence.

Can being gay or lesbian make you hate yourself?

It isn't your sexual orientation that causes you to hate yourself, it is the pressure from family, friends, and the larger community to change something that feels normal and natural for you. You might think something is wrong with you because of your sexual orientation, but these feelings reflect what you have been taught about gay and lesbian people. These thoughts are damaging to self-esteem and can cause depression. Feelings of worthlessness, of not being loved or important to anyone, of isolation from your family, of self-hatred, of loneliness, and of hopelessness can all lead to depression and even to suicidal thoughts. It is estimated that over 30 percent of all teens who commit suicide are gay or lesbian. Again, this is not because of gay teenagers' sexual orientation but because society forces them to grow up hiding and hating who they are.

Do churches and synagogues accept gay people?

Most Christian denominations have within their membership a gay movement, including American Baptist, Brethren/Mennonite, Catholic, Lutheran, Presbyterian, Unitarian, United Church of Christ, United Methodist,

Quaker, Evangelical, Mormon, and many others. Many large cities have gay Jewish congregations. In 1969, Reverend Troy Perry organized the Metropolitan Community Church of Los Angeles to serve gay men and lesbians. There are now over 250 MCC churches in the United States.

Some gay people gain a meaningful experience through religious worship with people who love and accept them. Gay people can also meet new friends and participate in social activities at their place of worship.

What does the Bible say about homosexuality?

It depends on who you talk with and how they interpret the Bible. Many theologians and church leaders say homosexuality is not wrong. Traditionally, organized religion has denounced gay and lesbian relationships because sex was supposed to be only for procreation (having children). The Bible has sometimes been used to justify persecution and discrimination against gays and other groups of people. Many passages in the Bible, however, teach people to love one another, to treat others with respect, and not to judge others. Although the Bible is sometimes used as a weapon against them, many gay men and lesbians still consider it a helpful guide in their lives.

CHAPTER FIVE

Coming Out

The yellow pages made a rippling sound as Nicki flipped through the telephone book. Office—Physicians—Printers—Restaurants—Signs—the words started to blur as she let the pages fall past her thumb. She stopped when she got to the page that said Social Services. Somewhere there should be a number for that center, Nicki mumbled to herself. She adjusted the book on her lap and leaned against the wall. She was determined to find the number. This wasn't the first time Nicki had thought about calling the center. She didn't know why she was so scared to call. All she wanted was information, and the person who answered the phone would not know who she was. But she kept putting it off. She lifted her eyes from the telephone book to watch her black cat, Buttons, poke her head through the bedroom door.

"Here, kitty, kitty," Nicki said softly. Buttons slowly walked toward Nicki. When she got close enough, Buttons nudged her head against the telephone book. Nicki wanted to hold Buttons close to her and listen to her purr. But Buttons jumped over to the chair where she could look out the window and watch the squirrels. Nicki laughed at the clicking sound that Buttons was making in her frustration at not being free to run outside and chase the birds and squirrels. "Just like me," Nicki thought, "never feeling free to be who I really am."

Nicki ran her fingers down the list of social service agencies. Finally she saw the listing for the Gay/Lesbian Hotline. She looked at the number, thinking about how she would start the conversation. "Hi, my name is Nicki. I am 16 years old and a lesbian." "Hello, can you tell me what kinds of things you do at the center?" Nicki continued to practice her opening sentence, changing the words and even the tone of her voice, but everything sounded phony.

Finally she went out to the hall, brought the phone into her room, and closed the door. She dialed the number and counted the rings—one—two—three. Nicki was nervous. She thought about hanging up before someone answered. "Hello, Gay and Lesbian Hotline, Dana speaking." The sound of the woman's voice made Nicki feel better, but she didn't say anything at first.

"Hello," Dana repeated.

"Hello, I have some questions I would like to ask someone. Is there someone I could talk with?"

"Yes, you can talk with me. My name is Dana."

"Hi Dana, my name is Nic—umm."

"That's okay, you don't have to tell me your name."

"I have so many questions, I just don't know where to begin. I guess I need to talk with someone who will understand how I feel. I haven't talked with my family and even my best friends don't know that I am a lesbian."

"You must feel very alone at times."

"Yeah! I do. I have really nice friends, but I'm not sure what they would think if I told them. My family would be so disappointed in me. It scares me to think of telling them. One minute I think they would understand and then the next minute I think—nope—they'll disown me."

"I understand how you feel. I used to feel the same way."

"Really? I thought I was the only one. What did you do? I mean, how did you finally get around to telling people?"

Nicki began to feel at ease as she listened to Dana talk about "coming out." Dana seemed to know just the right questions to ask, like how long had she known she was a lesbian, what books had she read about being gay, did she get along with her parents, how did she like school, and had she thought about why she wanted to tell people?

As Nicki and Dana continued to talk, Nicki looked up at Buttons near the window. Nicki made a silent promise to her cat: "Tomorrow, after I get home from school, I'll take you out to the backyard so you can find out what it feels like to be what you were meant to be!"

I think I am gay—who should I talk with?

First, be patient with yourself. It will probably take a while to come to understand and accept your sexual identity. Try not to allow the negative things that you may have heard about being gay or lesbian destroy the beauty and uniqueness of who you are.

Some communities, like the one Nicki lives in, have a gay and lesbian hotline that you can call. That phone number should be listed in the telephone book. If there is no hotline, contact the nearest Federation of Parents and Friends of Lesbians and Gays. The people there can give you information and direct you to other groups. There are organizations listed in the back of this book and also at your local library. The most important thing to remember is that whatever feelings you have, you are not crazy or mentally ill, and you are not alone.

What does "coming out of the closet" mean?

"Coming out of the closet" or "coming out" is a term used by lesbians and gay men that means telling other people that you are gay. The phrase reflects the way gay men and lesbians have had to hide their sexual identity. For some gay people, the process of coming out is easy. But for many, finding acceptance from their family and friends is difficult. Therefore, rather than face disapproval, ridicule, and harassment, they choose to stay silent. A very important part of themselves remains locked away, hidden from others. They are said to be "in the closet" or "closeted."

What questions should I ask myself before coming out?

The process of learning about and feeling comfortable with who we are sexually takes time. Sexuality involves more than just feeling physical pleasure. It encompasses our emotional and spiritual feelings also. It is common to feel confusion and uncertainty about who we are during the adolescent years. You may decide that "coming out to yourself" is the most important first step. Explore your own feelings and become comfortable with your sexuality before letting others know.

Following is a list of questions to ask yourself before you decide to let others know that you are gay:

Are you knowledgeable about homosexuality? Family and friends will want to ask you a lot of questions. It won't feel good to be bombarded with questions unless you feel secure about your answers.

Do you feel comfortable with your sexuality? If you see it as negative, your friends will also be more apt to think of it as negative.

Are you sure that you are gay? If you're confused, others might not believe you. Unless you're certain, it might be best to wait to tell others.

Has your relationship with your parents been generally good? If they have been willing to work through other issues with you in the past, then you can probably work through this together. However, if you feel they may throw you out of the house, withhold financial support, or in any way make life difficult for you, you would be wise to wait until you are more independent.

Remember, coming out to family and friends is a personal decision that only you can make. Do not let anyone pressure you into doing it before you are ready. Educate yourself, find emotional support and strength from others, and follow your own instincts. It is hard to predict how others will react, so choose who, when, where, and how carefully.

How can I find other gay kids to hang out with?

Some cities offer discussion groups and other youth programs within community centers. Many colleges and religious groups have gay and lesbian groups. Most large cities have an established gay community. Often there are sports groups, youth groups, and many kinds of social activities. In many big cities you can find a newspaper especially for gay people. There are also some national gay publications (see the resource list on page 55). These papers might have information about youth groups or about finding a pen pal.

The gay community is very diverse and encompasses people from a wide variety of backgrounds. There are groups for African-American, Hispanic, Jewish, and other ethnic gay people. Gay people of color face both homophobia and racism and sometimes feel pressure to choose to identify with either the ethnic community or with the gay community. Getting together and talking with other gay people of color is a way to deal with those issues.

Will dealing with my sexuality become easier?

Every adult in the world has survived the adolescent years, just as you are doing now. Many people—homosexual and heterosexual—have come to terms with who they are. Other adults continue to struggle with their identity. Usually it becomes easier to accept your sexual identity as you grow older. You will meet other gay people and realize you are not alone. You will also come to understand that being gay is not a hardship. It is like a special gift or talent that not everyone understands easily.

CHAPTER SIX

Healthy Sexuality

Mark sat on the steps in front of the library. He looked at his watch for the fourth time. Although it seemed like he had been waiting for hours, his watch reminded him that he had only been there for a little over ten minutes.

He moved his books out of the way as a boy and girl, with their arms wrapped around each other, walked up the steps toward the library door. Mark watched the couple smile at each other and giggle as they tried to squeeze through the door at the same time.

"How nice it must be," he thought, "to be able to openly show affection toward each other."

He thought of himself and Joey—how careful they had to be in public. Mark had known Joey for about a year. They met during their junior year in high school. They were both on the school track team and had become friends mostly by talking about track. Then they found other things they had in common, and their relationship had grown over time.

Mark would never forget the day when Joey asked him out on what they later agreed was their first "date." "Poor Joey," he thought, smiling. "He was so nervous when he asked me if I wanted to go to the film festival." Joey said that he had picked up the phone three times, only to lose his nerve and hang up. By the time he did call, his voice was cracking and the palms of his hands were sweaty. Mark had laughed, because he remembered that his older brother had gone through the same thing when he started to call girls.

Joey and Mark would be leaving for different colleges after the summer. This would be a special summer for them, and they were making plans for a camping trip, baseball games, and long bike rides.

Mark felt physically excited when he thought of being with Joey. What made him really happy was how comfortable the two were starting to feel when they held hands and kissed each other. They hadn't gone any farther yet, but they had talked about how they could make their sexual relationship a good—and safe—experience. Mark was looking forward to getting more involved with Joey, but he was also a little scared.

Mark stood up and looked across the lawn toward the parking lot. He caught a glimpse of Joey getting out of his car. The sight of Joey always made him feel happy. His instinct was to run toward him and throw his arms around his neck, but instead he whistled to get Joey's attention.

Joey took the steps two at a time. He gave Mark a friendly punch on the arm, and they started through the door, laughing and smiling at each other.

"We aren't much different than the couple who walked through here a few minutes ago," Mark said.

"What did you say?" asked Joey.

"Oh, nothing," Mark said, grinning.

Discovering your sexuality and learning about yourself as a sexual human being is an important part of becoming a whole person. Learning how to give and receive love through physical closeness can be one of life's most rewarding experiences. But being ready to be sexually active means more than just being ready physically. Sex involves people emotionally as well.

Building a good relationship takes patience and the willingness to spend time getting to know your partner. As you grow close to someone, there are many ways to show affection besides having sexual contact. Taking walks, hugging, kissing, helping each other with schoolwork, talking about each other's goals are all ways of showing affection. Healthy affection is based on respect for another person. Four values to think about when you are involved in a relationship—they can be referred to as the four "R's"— are *respect, responsibility, reaction,* and *restraint.*

First, respect. If you respect and view yourself as a good and worthwhile person—in other words, you have self-respect—others around you will pick up on those feelings. Respect for your partner is also an important part of a healthy relationship. Second, responsibility. Being responsible means thinking about the consequences of your actions before you do something. Many of the choices you make now will affect your future. Third, our reactions to sexual feelings are important. Sexual feelings are energy. Healthy sexuality means channeling that energy so that we and our partners feel physically, emotionally, and spiritually well. Last, restraint. We are all capable of restraining ourselves and not acting on every thought or feeling. Pressuring others to act on sexual feelings before they are ready hurts you and those you care about.

Many adolescents choose to delay sexual activity. This gives them time to develop other aspects of their identity. Many adolescents just don't feel ready for sexual activity in their high school years. Another reason for delaying sexual activity is because of the health risks. In the United States, every 13 seconds a teen gets a sexually transmitted disease. As of 1991, more than 32,000 people between the ages of 20 and 29 were diagnosed with AIDS. Many of these people probably were infected during adolescence. Heterosexual and homosexual adolescents are at risk of getting AIDS and other sexually transmitted diseases, but knowing the facts can help you ensure a healthy future.

What is AIDS?

AIDS stands for *A*cquired *I*mmuno*d*eficiency *S*yndrome. AIDS is caused by the virus called human immunodeficiency virus, or HIV. (A virus is a small organism that causes disease.) The HIV virus breaks down the body's immune system—the system that fights off infection. When the immune system breaks down, the body is unable to overcome illnesses. For example, if your immune system is not in order, a simple cold can turn into pneumonia.

How do people get infected with the HIV virus?

The HIV virus is passed from one person to another

through the bloodstream. This can happen by engaging in vaginal or anal intercourse with a person who already has HIV, by sharing drug needles or syringes with an infected person, or, very rarely, through a blood transfusion. Women who are infected with HIV can also pass the virus on to their babies during pregnancy, birth, or possibly by breast-feeding.

During sexual intercourse with an infected person, the virus can get into the bloodstream of an uninfected person through cuts or sores on the vagina, penis, or rectum and possibly through the mouth. The exchange of infected blood, semen, or vaginal secretions spreads the virus. The more sexual partners you have, the higher your risk of being in contact with someone who is infected. Taking birth control pills does not protect you from the virus.

People with HIV cannot pass the virus to others through touching, hugging, kissing, using the same dishes, swimming, or holding hands. Nor can you get it from mosquitoes or other insects.

Do gay men have a high risk of getting AIDS?

At the beginning of the AIDS crisis, most of the people who contracted AIDS were gay men and intravenous (IV) drug users. The disease has since spread to the population at large, including heterosexual men and women. Gay men are still considered at high risk for getting the disease, but just because you are a gay man does not mean you will get AIDS.

Gay men have taken the leadership role in the fight against AIDS. They have organized groups to get funding for research, have established clinics and support groups, and have been active in generating national awareness of the disease.

There have been very few documented cases of female-to-female transmission of the AIDS virus. Still, lesbians are at risk of getting the virus, like everyone else.

How can I keep from getting AIDS?

The only sure guarantee for the prevention of AIDS or other sexually transmitted diseases is abstaining from sexual intercourse. It is also important to stay away from drugs of any kind. Any drug, including alcohol, impairs your ability to make good decisions. When you're under the influence of a drug, you might decide to have unsafe sex.

What can I do if I want to be sexually active?

If you feel you are ready to handle the responsibility of having a sexual relationship, there are some questions you should ask your partner: have you had any sexually transmitted diseases? How many sexual partners have you had? Are you taking illegal drugs now or have you ever in the past? If these questions seem too personal or embarrassing to talk about with your partner, then perhaps you are not ready to take on the responsibility of having a sexual relationship.

You can decrease your chances of getting HIV or other sexually transmitted diseases by using condoms. Use condoms made of latex rubber only, as it serves as a barrier to the virus. Place spermicide in the tip of the condom and put the condom on as soon as the penis becomes erect. If the condom breaks during intercourse, do not continue until you have put on a new condom. After intercourse, while the penis is still erect, withdraw while holding the rim of the condom. Do not wash out and reuse the condom.

What other sexually transmitted diseases do I have to worry about?

There are more than 20 different sexually transmitted diseases. Because there is no cure for AIDS at this time, we hear about it more than some of the others. But gonorrhea, syphilis, herpes, and chlamydia can be very serious and can cause heart disease, infertility, or sterility.

Healthy sexuality can bring us great pleasure and rewards, but, like everything else that is worthwhile in life, it does not come easily or without self-discipline and respect for ourselves and others.

CONCLUSION

The journey from childhood to adulthood is never easy. We want to be free from our parents' rules—free to explore the benefits of being an adult. Yet our self-esteem during this time is still largely based on what others think or feel about us. Therefore, the pressure to conform is intense. It may seem safe to conform to the values of a particular group, but giving in to peer pressure can threaten your unique potential. This is true for all adolescents, but especially for those who are outside of what is considered the "normal" mainstream.

It takes a brave person to do something that others may object to, and in our society, many people object to others being gay or lesbian. We are told from a very early age that there is something wrong with loving someone of the same gender. Many of us can see how ridiculous it is to judge people because they choose to love someone of their own sex, but others cause great emotional and physical harm to gays and lesbians.

It is up to each of us to do our part in creating an atmosphere of safety for all people. Homophobia perpetuates violence, and violence against any group of people affects each of us. Name-calling, jokes about, and harassment of people we view as different are very damaging. If we stand in silence and watch others do these things, we are saying by our silence that it is all right to be violent towards others.

Resources

Organizations

American Friends Service Committee
1501 Cherry Street
Philadelphia, PA 19102

Gay and Lesbian Youth Advocacy Council
55 Mason Street
San Francisco, CA 94102

Lambda Legal Defense and Education Fund
666 Broadway
New York, NY 10012

National Coalition of Advocates for Students
100 Boylston Street, Suite 737
Boston, MA 02116

National Federation of Parents and Friends of Gays
8020 Eastern Avenue NW
Washington, D.C. 20012

National Gay Alliance of Young Adults
P.O. Box 190426
Dallas, TX 75219-0426

National Gay and Lesbian Resource Center
Fund for Human Dignity
666 Broadway, Suite 410
New York, NY 10012

National Gay and Lesbian Task Force
1517 U Street NW
Washington, D.C. 20009

National Gay Youth Network
P.O. Box 846
San Francisco, CA 94101

National Lesbian/Gay Health Foundation
1638 R Street NW, Suite 2
Washington, D.C. 20009

National Network of Runaway and Youth Services
1400 I Street NW, Suite 330
Washington, D.C. 20005

Parents FLAG
P.O. Box 20308
Denver, CO 80220

The Universal Fellowship of Metropolitan Community Churches
5300 Santa Monica Boulevard
Los Angeles, CA 90029

National Telephone Hotlines

AIDS Hotline
1-800-342-AIDS

National Gay and Lesbian Crisis Line
1-800-SOS-GAYS

Sexually-Transmitted Diseases National Hotline
1-800-227-8922

If you would like to correspond with a gay or lesbian teenager, you can send your letter to Alyson Publications and they will put you in touch with a pen pal.
Write: **Letter Exchange**
      Alyson Publications
      40 Plympton Street
      Boston, MA 02118

For Further Reading

Nonfiction

The Alyson Almanac. Boston: Alyson Publications, 1989.

Alyson, Sasha, ed. Young, Gay, and Proud. Boston: Alyson Publications, 1980.

Back, Gloria Guss. Are You Still My Mother? Are You Still My Family? New York: Warner Books, 1985.

Beam, Joseph, ed. In the Life. Boston: Alyson Publications, 1986.

Bell, Ruth, et. al. Changing Bodies, Changing Lives: A Book for Teens on Sex and Relationships. New York: Random House, 1988.

Berzon, Betty, ed. Positively Gay. Los Angeles: Mediamix Associates, 1979.

Bullough, Vern L. Homosexuality: A History. New York: New American Library, 1979.

Clark, Don. The New Loving Someone Gay. Berkeley, CA: Celestial Arts, 1987.

Cohen, Susan, and Daniel Cohen. When Someone You Know Is Gay. New York: M. Evans, 1989.

Fairchild, Betty, and Nancy Hayward. Now That You Know: What Every Parent Should Know about Homosexuality. San Diego: Harcourt Brace Jovanovich, 1981.

Fricke, Aaron. Reflections of a Rock Lobster: A Story about Growing up Gay. Boston: Alyson Publications, 1981.

Hanckel, Frances, and John Cunningham. *A Way of Love, a Way of Life: A Young Person's Introduction to What It Means to Be Gay.* New York: Lothrop, Lee & Shepard Books, 1979.

Heron, Ann, ed. *One Teenager in Ten: Writings by Gay and Lesbian Youth.* Boston: Alyson Publications, 1983.

Holbrook, Sabra. *Fighting Back: The Struggle for Gay Rights.* New York: E.P. Dutton, 1987.

Landau, Elaine. *Different Drummer: Homosexuality in America.* New York: Julian Messner, 1986.

Muller, Ann. *Parents Matter: Parents' Relationships with Lesbian Daughters and Gay Sons.* Tallahassee, Florida: Naiad Press, 1987.

Rench, Janice E. *Teen Sexuality: Decisions and Choices.* Minneapolis: Lerner Publications Company, 1988.

Rofes, Eric E. *"I Thought People Like That Killed Themselves": Lesbians, Gay Men and Suicide.* San Francisco: Gray Fox Press, 1983.

Whitlock, Katherine. *Bridges of Respect: Creating Support for Lesbian and Gay Youth.* Philadelphia: American Friends Service Committee, 1988.

Fiction

Bradley, Marion Zimmer. *The Catch Trap*. New York: Ballantine Books, 1979.

Brown, Rita Mae. *Rubyfruit Jungle*. New York: Bantam Books, 1977.

Garden, Nancy. *Annie on My Mind*. New York: Farrar, Straus and Giroux, 1982.

Hall, Lynn. *Sticks and Stones*. New York: Dell Books, 1972.

Homes, A.M. *Jack*. New York: Macmillan Publishing Company, 1989.

Klein, Norma. *Breaking Up*. New York: Pantheon, 1980.

Miller, Isabel. *Patience and Sarah*. New York: Fawcett Books, 1976.

Scoppettone, Sandra. *Happy Endings Are All Alike*. New York: Harper and Row, 1978.

Warren, Patricia Nell. *The Front Runner*. New York: Bantam Books, 1975.

Some national gay publications include *The Advocate, Christopher Street, Gay Community News,* and *Out/Look.*

INDEX